Beginning
To Read

E B

Brimner, Larry Dane

Cats!

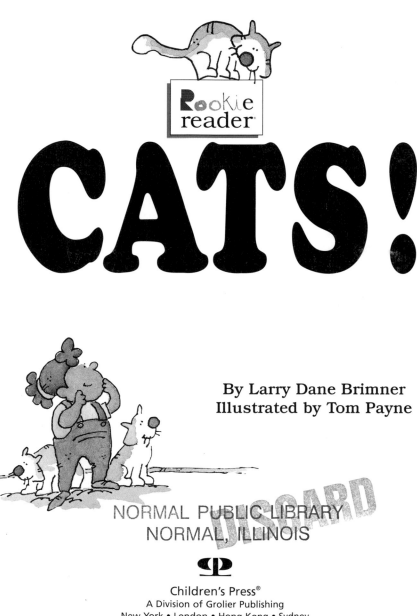

Rookie reader®

CATS!

By Larry Dane Brimner
Illustrated by Tom Payne

Children's Press®
A Division of Grolier Publishing
New York • London • Hong Kong • Sydney
Danbury, Connecticut

For my friends at West Sedona Elementary School
—L. D. B.

Reading Consultants
Linda Cornwell
Coordinator of School Quality and Professional Improvement
(Indiana State Teachers Association)

Katharine A. Kane
Education Consultant
(Retired, San Diego County Office of Education
and San Diego State University)

Visit Children's Press® on the Internet at:
http://publishing.grolier.com

Library of Congress Cataloging-in-Publication Data
Brimner, Larry Dane.
    Cats! / by Larry Dane Brimner ; illustrated by Tom Payne.
        p. cm. — (Rookie reader)
    Summary: A child has fun playing with some cats.
    ISBN 0-516-22010-1 (lib. bdg.)   0-516-27075-3 (pbk.)
    [1. Cats—Fiction.] I. Payne, Tom, ill. II. Title. III. Series.
PZ7.B767 Cat 2000
[E]— dc21   99-057169

GROLIER
PUBLISHING

Cats!

Come in, cats.

Let's play, cats.

Please, cats!
Stay on the floor.

9

Don't swing, cats.

11

Don't fight, cats.

13

No, cats!
Don't scratch the door.

What's this, cats?
A string, cats.

Catch it, cats—
if you can.

Close, cats.
Almost, cats.

Oh, silly cats!
I love you more and more.

Word List (33 words)

a	floor	play
almost	I	please
and	if	scratch
can	in	silly
catch	it	stay
cats	let's	string
close	love	swing
come	more	the
don't	no	this
door	oh	what's
fight	on	you

About the Author

Larry Dane Brimner writes and writes and writes. Among his Rookie Reader titles for Children's Press are *How Many Ants?*, *Cowboy Up!*, and *Raindrops*. When he isn't writing, Larry is probably snoozing at his California home or rollerblading along the beach.

About the Illustrator

Tom Payne has been a humorous illustrator for a very long time. His work has appeared in all sorts of books and magazines. He commutes into his studio, which he shares with some other "arty" people, in Albany, New York, from his home in the nearby Helderberg Mountains. He lives with his wife, Anne, and his son, Thomas.